CAVING

BY JACK DAVID

BELLWETHER MEDIA • MINNEAPOLIS, MN

Are you ready to take it to the extreme? Torque books thrust you into the action-packed world of sports, vehicles, and adventure. These books may include dirt, smoke, fire, and dangerous stunts. WARNING: Read at your own risk.

This edition first published in 2009 by Bellwether Media.

No part of this publication may be reproduced in whole or in part without written permission of the publisher. For information regarding permission, write to Bellwether Media Inc., Attention: Permissions Department, Post Office Box 19349, Minneapolis, MN 55419.

Library of Congress Cataloging-in-Publication Data
David, Jack, 1968–
  Caving / by Jack David.
    p. cm. — (Torque : action sports)
  Summary: "Photographs of amazing feats accompany engaging information about Caving. The combination of high-interest subject matter and light text is intended for readers in grades 3 through 7"—Provided by publisher.
  Includes bibliographical references and index.
  ISBN-13: 978-1-60014-199-7 (hardcover : alk. paper)
  ISBN-10: 1-60014-199-4 (hardcover : alk. paper)
  1. Caving—Juvenile literature. I. Title.

GV200.62.D38 2009
796.52'5—dc22   2008016608

CONTENTS

WHAT IS CAVING?

Hidden below the earth's surface lies a dark and exciting world. Caves are one of the world's last unexplored areas. They're full of beautiful rock formations, crystal-clear lakes, rushing rivers, and strange animals. Few people ever see these wonders, but cavers know them well.

Caving is a sport that combines adventure, exploration, and hard work. Cavers use lights, ropes, and other gear to explore and map these strange underground worlds. It's a sport that demands patience, responsibility, and plenty of courage. It also offers a unique experience that no other sport can match.

EQUIPMENT

Many **show caves** can be explored without special gear. Show caves are set up with lights and marked paths. They're perfect for tourists. However, skilled cavers like to explore **wild caves**. This requires some basic equipment.

Every caver needs a helmet. Helmets are important to protect cavers in small areas and from falling rocks. They also have a mount for a light. A hands-free light is important when a caver needs both hands to crawl in or climb a difficult part of a cave.

Light is important for finding your way in a dark cave. Cavers always bring at least three light sources in case two of them fail. Heavy-duty flashlights are common. Some cavers also carry lamps that burn a chemical called **carbide**.

Ropes help cavers move up and down the steep sections of a cave. Cavers attach themselves to their ropes with **harnesses**. A harness fits around a caver's waist and legs. It attaches to the rope with a clip called a **carabiner**. Ropes attach to the rock by tools called **anchors**.

Climbers also need proper clothing. Caves are full of sharp, jagged rocks. The air underground can be much colder than the air on the surface. Long pants and long sleeves keep cavers warm and protect them from sharp rocks. Soft leather gloves protect the hands and ankle-high boots protect the feet.

CAVING IN ACTION

Cavers need to use different skills in each cave. Some caves require a lot of crawling to get through narrow tunnels. Some even force cavers to creep along in a **belly crawl.**

Cavers have to use their ropes to move up and down in some caves. In others, they use a technique called **scrambling**. Scrambling is a cross between climbing and crawling, used on steep, rocky slopes. Climbers use a technique called **squeezing** to get through very narrow openings.

fast fact

Potholing is a type of
caving that involves
deep vertical caves.
These caves go almost
straight down.

Many cavers make maps as they explore. They may try to map unexplored parts of caves. They may also look for a connection between two caves.

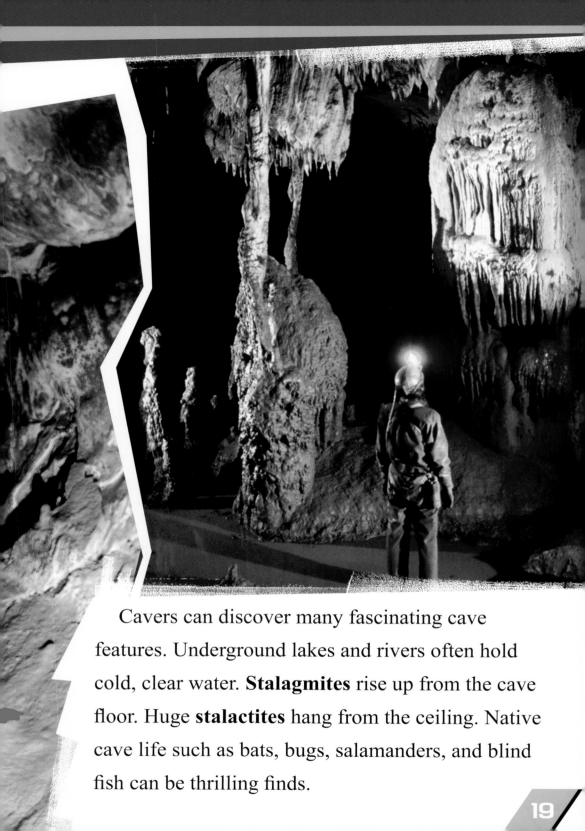

Cavers can discover many fascinating cave features. Underground lakes and rivers often hold cold, clear water. **Stalagmites** rise up from the cave floor. Huge **stalactites** hang from the ceiling. Native cave life such as bats, bugs, salamanders, and blind fish can be thrilling finds.

Responsible cavers are careful not to disturb these fragile wonders. The caver's motto is: "Take nothing but pictures. Leave nothing but footprints. Kill nothing but time." It reminds cavers to leave caves just the way they found them, for others to enjoy.

GLOSSARY

anchor—a tool that secures a rope to a rock

belly crawl—a caving technique in which a climber gets all the way down on his or her belly to inch along a cave floor

carabiner—an oblong metal clip often used to fasten people to ropes for climbing

carbide—a chemical that cavers use as lamp fuel

harness—a set of straps worn around the waist and legs; a harness is used to secure a person to a rope.

scramble—a caving technique that involves climbing up a slope on all fours

show cave—a cave that has been prepared for viewing, with lighting, marked paths, and other safety features

squeezing—a caving technique in which a caver slips through a narrow opening

stalactite—a cone-shaped piece of rock that hangs from the ceiling of a cave

stalagmite—a cone-shaped piece of rock that rises up from a cave floor

wild cave—a cave that hasn't been specially prepared with lights, paths, or other safety features

TO LEARN MORE

AT THE LIBRARY

Brimner, Larry Dane. *Caving: Exploring Limestone Caves*. New York: Franklin Watts, 2001.

Green, Emily K. *Caves*. Minneapolis, Minn.: Bellwether, 2007.

Howes, Chris. *Caving*. Chicago, Ill.: Heinemann, 2003.

ON THE WEB

Learning more about caving is as easy as 1, 2, 3.

1. Go to www.factsurfer.com
2. Enter "caving" into search box.
3. Click the "Surf" button and you will see a list of related web sites.

With factsurfer.com, finding more information is just a click away.

INDEX